Class 2

I Know That!

Plastic

Claire Llewellyn

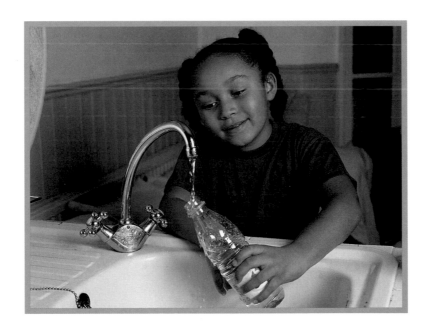

W
FRANKLIN WATTS
LONDON • SYDNEY

First published in 2004
by Franklin Watts
96 Leonard Street
London EC2A 4XD

Franklin Watts Australia
45-51 Huntley Street
Alexandria, NSW 2015

Series advisor: Gill Matthews, non-fiction literacy
consultant and Inset trainer
Editor: Rachel Cooke
Series design: Peter Scoulding
Designer: James Marks
Photography: Ray Moller unless otherwise credited
Acknowledgements: Mark Antman /The Image Works/Topham: 14. Nick Cobbing/Still Pictures: 20.
Lauren Goodsmith/Image Works/Topham: 13t. Philippe Psaila/SPL: 16. Helene Rogers/Art
Directors/Trip:12. Joe Sohm/Image Works/Topham: 15l.
Thanks to our models Jaydee Cozzi, Jakob Hawker, Hayley Sapsford and Phoebus Zavros

A CIP catalogue record for this book is available from the British Library.

ISBN: 0 7496 5722 7

Printed in Malaysia

Contents

Plastic is useful

Plastic is a very useful material. All sorts of things are made of plastic.

▼ *These things are all made of plastic.*

Food box

Comb

Sponge

Bangle

4

Bag

Can you think of three other things that are made of plastic?

Bottle

Toy

Cup

Ruler

Toothbrush

Watch

5

All kinds of plastic

There are many different kinds of plastic.

▶ *Plastic can be soft and bendy...*

▶ *or hard and stiff.*

▶ *Plastic can be squashy...*

▼ *or stretchy.*

▼ *It can be colourful...*

What kinds of plastic have been used to make these swimming goggles?

◀ *or clear.*

7

Plastic is strong

Plastic does not break easily.
It is very strong.

A plastic bottle does not break when you drop it.

This plastic basket holds a lot of washing.

Have a look round your home. What things are made of plastic?

Plastic things can be used over and over again.

9

Plastic is waterproof

Water cannot get through plastic. It is a waterproof material.

Hood

Coat

Umbrella

Boots

► *Plastic things keep you dry in the rain.*

▼ *You can move water around in plastic.*

Pour some drops of water on a paper towel. Now pour some drops on a plastic bag. What happens to the water?

Plastic is easy to look after

Plastic is easy to look after.
It does not need a lot of care.

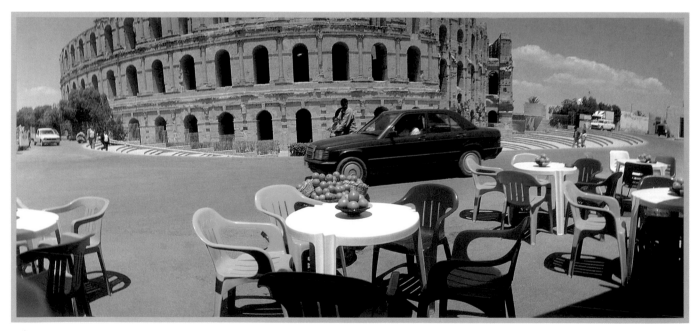

Plastic chairs and tables do not rot.

Plastic toys never go rusty.

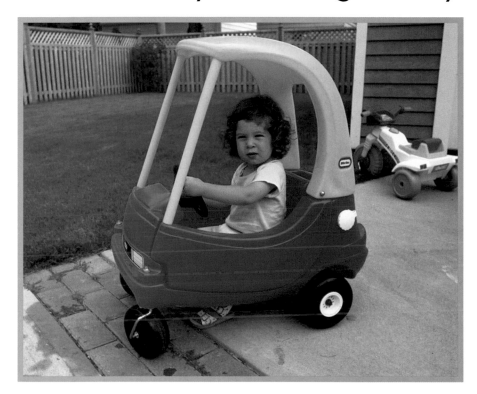

Many outdoor things are made of plastic. How many can you spot at school?

This plastic-covered cloth is easy to clean.

Plastic is made from oil

People make plastic from oil.

Plastic is not a natural material. It is made by people, not by nature.

▲ *Black, sticky oil is found under the ground.*

The oil is taken to a big factory.

Some of the oil is used to make tiny plastic chips.

Shaping plastic

Plastic melts when it is heated. It can then be made into different shapes.

► *This is a mould for making plastic bricks. Melted plastic has been poured into it.*

As the plastic cooled it went hard. It has kept the brick shape of the mould.

We pour hot, runny jelly into a mould. What happens as the jelly cools?

These things were made in moulds.

Wearing plastic

Hot plastic can be pulled into long, thin threads. These are used to make cloth.

▼ *All these clothes were made from plastic.*

Soft, stretchy jumper

Soft, fluffy fleece

Do you think any of your clothes are made from plastic?

Smooth, strong skirt

Smooth, stretchy tights

19

Plastic makes rubbish

A lot of plastic ends up as rubbish.
We must try to throw less away.

► *Look at all the plastic in this bin.*

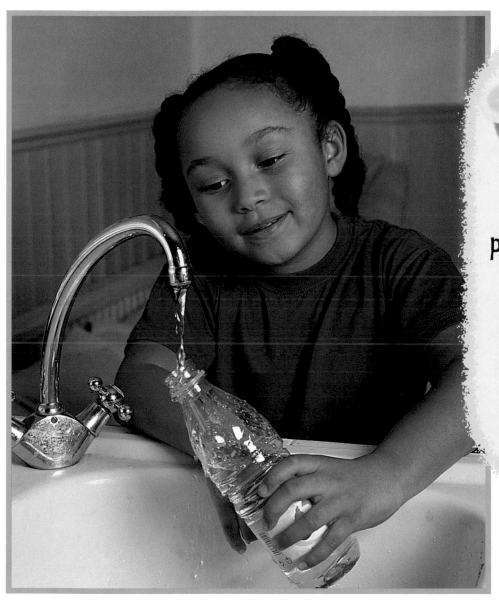

These empty plastic tubs and pots are too useful to be rubbish. How could you use them again?

Don't throw away a plastic bottle! Use it again.

I know that...

1 Plastic is useful.

2 There are many kinds of plastic

3 Plastic is strong.

4 Plastic is waterproof.

5 Plastic is easy to look after.

6 Plastic is made from oil.

7 Plastic can be shaped when it is melted. It goes hard when it is cool.

8 Plastic is used to make cloth.

9 We must try to throw away less plastic.

23

Index

About this book

I Know That! is designed to introduce children to the process of gathering information and using reference books, one of the key skills needed to begin more formal learning at school. For this reason, each book's structure reflects the information books children will use later in their learning career – with key information in the main text and additional facts and ideas in the captions. The panels give an opportunity for further activities, ideas or discussions. The contents page and index are helpful reference guides.

The language is carefully chosen to be accessible to children just beginning to read. Illustrations support the text but also give information in their own right; active consideration and discussion of images is another key referencing skill. The main aim of the series is to build confidence – showing children how much they already know and giving them the ability to gather new information for themselves. With this in mind, the *I know that...* section at the end of the book is a simple way for children to revisit what they already know as well as what they have learnt from reading the book.